Walk Around
Hawker Hurricane

By Ron MacKay

Color by Don Greer

Illustrated by Ernesto Cumpian and David W. Smith

Walk Around Number 14

squadron/signal publications

Introduction

The history of the Hawker Hurricane deserves far more coverage than has been the case to date. Its prime importance to RAF Fighter Command, particularly during the crucial Battle of Britain, tends to be ignored or downplayed in the face of its contemporary, the Supermarine Spitfire. This is not surprising because the advanced shape of the 'Spit' has tended to place the more pedestrian layout of the Hurricane in the shade. Additionally, the Spitfire Fund was created during World War II with no similar War Savings program covering the 'Hurri'. Another distorting influence lies with the media which still has a love affair with Supermarine's creation even into the 1990s. Nevertheless, interest in the Hurricane has grown in recent years. Previously, the number of airworthy Hurricanes was very small in comparison to the Spitfire, but it is now possible to see up to four of Sir Sydney Camm's designs in the air together.

This book utilizes no less than five preserved aircraft with which to demonstrate the aircraft's salient points. The early Mark I (Mk 1) with fabric-covered wings located at the Science Museum, London was an ideal starting point. Access to the Duxford-based Sea Hurricane from the Shuttleworth Collection was a real bonus since this aircraft is virtually a complete example of a World War II Mk I. By comparison, the Mk XIIB of The Fighter Collection has several basic features which are Post-war adaptations. Nevertheless, this particular aircraft serves to illustrate the (admittedly limited) development of the design. Finally, the cannon-armed Mk IICs from the Battle of Britain Memorial Flight are included (including one under restoration at the Historic Aircraft Company following its fiery crash-landing several years ago) and the example preserved at RAF Cosford's museum. In this manner, the basic range of Hurricane variations has been thoroughly examined.

Acknowledgements

My eternal gratitude is expressed to Norman Chapman, a WW II and Post-war aircraft engineer. His detailed knowledge of Hawker's superb fighter has proved invaluable in assembling the material for the HURRICANE WALK AROUND. My thanks also to Colin Francis for his photographic skills, Steve McManus for access to the Sea Hurricane, and Clive Denny (Historic Flying) for similar access to the Mk IIC which his company is re-building. Equally worthy of mention is the sizable team from the Fighter Collection; in particular my thanks go to Andy Height and Danny Morris among their number who gave me full access to the Collection's Mk XII Hurricane.

PHOTO CREDITS
Ken Wixey
Ian Arnold
Bruce Robertson
Jerry Scutts
Enzio Maio

Dedication

This book is dedicated to the pilots and groundcrew who flew and serviced what was one of the most outstanding fighter aircraft ever to enter Royal Air Force service and which fought in every Theater of Operations from 3 September 1939 until 6 August 1945

ISBN 0-89747-388-4

If you have any photographs of aircraft, armor, soldiers or ships of any nation, particularly wartime snapshots, why not share them with us and help make Squadron/Signal's books all the more interesting and complete in the future. Any photograph sent to us will be copied and the original returned. The donor will be fully credited for any photos used. Please send them to:

Squadron/Signal Publications, Inc.
1115 Crowley Drive
Carrollton, TX 75011-5010

Если у вас есть фотографии самолётов, вооружения, солдат или кораблей любой страны, особенно, снимки времён войны, поделитесь с нами и помогите сделать новые книги издательства Эскадрон/Сигнал ещё интереснее. Мы переснимем ваши фотографии и вернём оригиналы. Имена приславших снимки будут сопровождать все опубликованные фотографии. Пожалуйста, присылайте фотографии по адресу:

Squadron/Signal Publications, Inc.
1115 Crowley Drive
Carrollton, TX 75011-5010

軍用機、装甲車両、兵士、軍艦などの写真を所持しておられる方はいらっしゃいませんか？どの国のものでも結構です。作戦中に撮影されたものが特に良いのです。Squadron/Signal社の出版する刊行物において、このような写真は内容を一層充実し、興味深くすることができます。当方にお送り頂いた写真は、複写の後お返しいたします。出版物中に写真を使用した場合は、必ず提供者のお名前を明記させて頂きます。お写真は下記にご送付ください。

Squadron/Signal Publications, Inc.
1115 Crowley Drive
Carrollton, TX 75011-5010

(Front Cover) Ju~B, a Hurricane Mk 1a (L2001) of 'A' Flight, 111 Squadron, RAF, provides air cover to British shipping in the English Channel just prior to the Battle of Britain in June of 1940.

(Back Cover) A Hurricane Mk IIa (Z3658, YO~N) of No. 401 Squadron, RCAF undergoes engine tests. Two crewmen had to sit on the tail to keep it down during full power run-ups.

(Above) The prototype Hurricane used an 11 foot, 3 inch diameter Watts two-bladed propeller. The landing gear cover comprises two linked sections with hinged doors on the lower section to fully enclose the gear as well as create an undisturbed flow of air into the radiator bath. The stabilizers are supported by bracing struts.

(Below) K5083 was the prototype Hurricane. The cockpit has a single vertical stiffener and the rudder line runs the full length of the fin. The radiator bath has a short divergent and convergent pattern. The exhaust ports are simple outlets in the cowling. While a number of small changes were made, the basic outline would remain unchanged on subsequent production aircraft.

(Above) The original radiator bath was short and rectangular in shape. The production model would be longer and feature an oval scoop. No guns were carried, but the wings were ballasted to compensate for their absence. The metal panels were brightly polished, while the fabric surfaces were coated with silver dope.

Camouflage Patterns

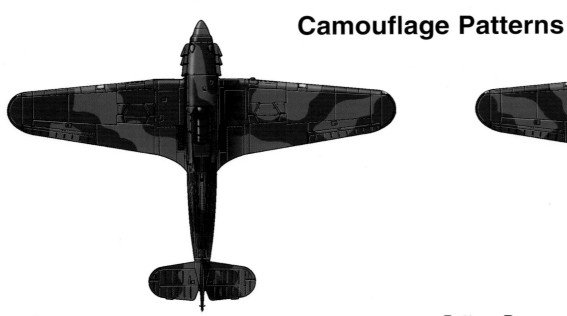

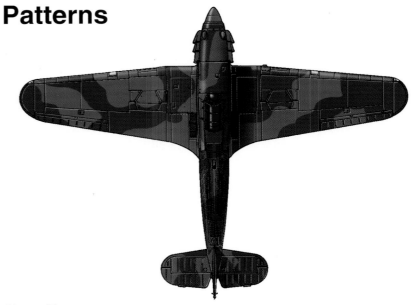

Pattern A

Pattern B

Royal Air Force and Navy Insignia

Type A Roundel

Type A.1 Roundel

Type B Roundel

Type C Roundel

Type C.1 Roundel

SEAC Roundel

L1592 is a Hurricane Mk I from the first production batch and has been preserved in the Science Museum in London, England. One of the external features of this production batch was the untapered radio mast. The fitting was superseded by tapered masts introduced during the second Mk 1 production batch. The aircraft joined 56 Squadron, in May of 1938, but bears the markings from its final operational unit — No. 615 (County of Surrey) Sqdn.

The Hurricane's original wings were fabric covered and the gun bay was covered by a single cross-shaped hatch with a separate rectangular hatch behind it. Three hinges secure the aileron to the wing. The detachable panel at the rear of the roundel provides access to the aileron cables.

The first three-bladed propeller fitted to the Hurricane was a De Havilland unit featuring a Hamilton Standard metal propeller with two pitch positions and a diameter of 10 feet 8 inches. The spinner is secured to its backplate by three screws between each propeller blade.

The two detachable panels under the rear fuselage consist of spruce formers and stringers covered in fabric. The rearmost unit has a plywood ventral fairing along its center-line which fairs in the tail wheel strut and joins the base of the rudder.

The horizontal stabilizers and elevators are fabric covered metal frames apart from the metal nosing strip on the stabilizer's leading edge. Fixed trim tabs extend beyond the elevator trailing edges.

(Above) The first Production Hurricane Mk I reveals several alterations from the prototype. The cockpit canopy now has two vertical stiffeners and the landing gear covers form one continuous pattern. The aircraft is equipped with kidney-shaped exhaust pipes, a flight gyro-instrument venturi mounted under the windshield, and an untapered radio mast located behind the cockpit. The pitot mast under the port wing is forked, but would be changed to an L-shaped unit on later production Mk Is.

(Below) RAF War Exercises were held in August of 1939 which accounts for some of 85 Sqdn's groundcrew wearing helmets and gas respirator bags. All three Hurricanes have Watts propellers, but none are fitted with armored windshields. The nearest is among the first to be built without the venturi below the windscreen. A few weeks later, on 3 September 1939, the steel helmets were for real.

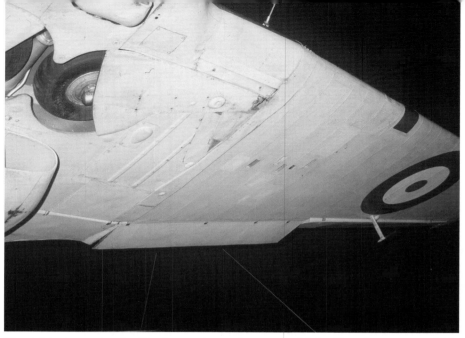

The original covering for Hurricane wing surfaces was fabric. The wings were quickly changed to metal stress-skinned wings with many early 'Hurris' being retrofitted after leaving the factory. L1592 went through its entire operational service (which culminated in the Battle of Britain) with fabric covered wings.

The flaps were divided into two sections with a total of six hinges. A separate hinged metal plate covered the V-shaped gap between the flap sections.

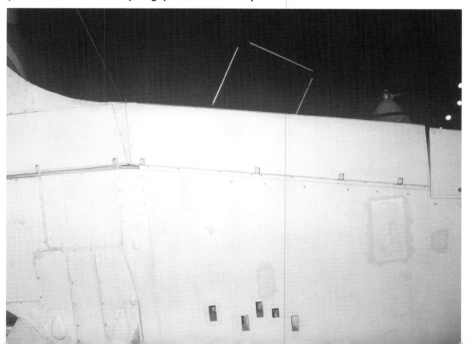

This Hurricane Mk I was one of 12 sold to Yugoslavia during 1939. The cartridge ejection chutes are covered with wing fabric. The faint diagonal lines on the wings denote the seams of the fabric which was applied in four foot widths. The wing join fairings are painted black. Also prominent are the two aft ventral fuselage panels.

The underside of the fabric covered aileron has three drain holes along its leading edge. These holes prevented the retention of moisture, thereby increasing the fabric's service life.

The landing gear in the retracted position reveals the extent to which the wheels were left uncovered in flight. The two strips behind the landing gear are stiffeners for the lower wing surfaces to counter buffeting when lowering the landing gear. They are secured by four and three screws on the inner and outer units respectively.

The lower fairing over the outer wing panel joints have a similar pattern to that on the upper surface, but only extends to the front face of the flap hinge line. The bolt connecting the landing gear radius rod cover to the main cover is hidden below the circular bulge on the gear cover. The egg-shaped bulge covers the fuel tank sump.

Production Hurricanes dispensed with wheel covers and left a portion of the wheel and tire exposed. Immediately in front of the wheel bay is the air intake leading to the engine's updraft carburetor. Behind the wheel bay is the face of the coolant radiator. A coolant pipe from the radiator to the engine is visible between the wheels.

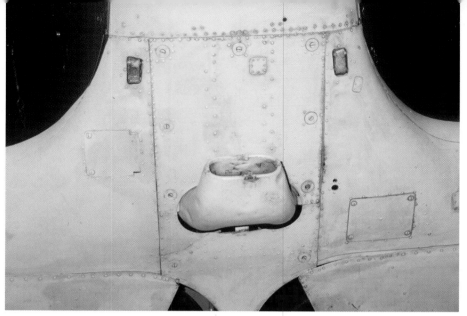

A jack support point is located on each side of the fuselage at the forward edge of the wing root fairing. The square panel above the starboard landing gear covers the Auxiliary Power Unit (APU) receptacle. Access to the fuel filter unit is via the square panel directly in front of the port landing gear. Many Hurricane's had a small mesh screen in the carburetor intake to keep out debris kicked up by the propeller.

The downward identification light, behind the radiator bath, is flanked by the emergency landing flare chute door. The lower aft surface of the radiator cover was a hinged flap controlled by the pilot. Opening the flap allowed a greater volume of air through the radiator and improved engine cooling.

A single bracing strut was centered inside the front of the radiator scoop. A mesh screen often protected the face of the radiator. The wheel wells have been left in natural metal.

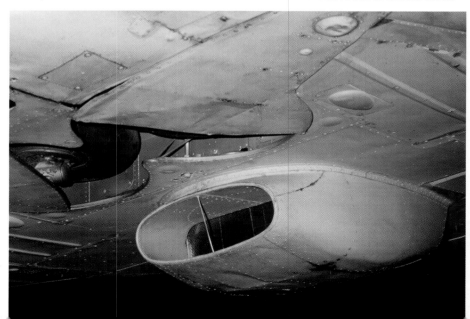

The center panel of the radiator bath provides access to the radiator and oil cooler drain plugs. The non-return valves between the main fuel tanks are accessed through the small circular ports just ahead of the radiator bath.

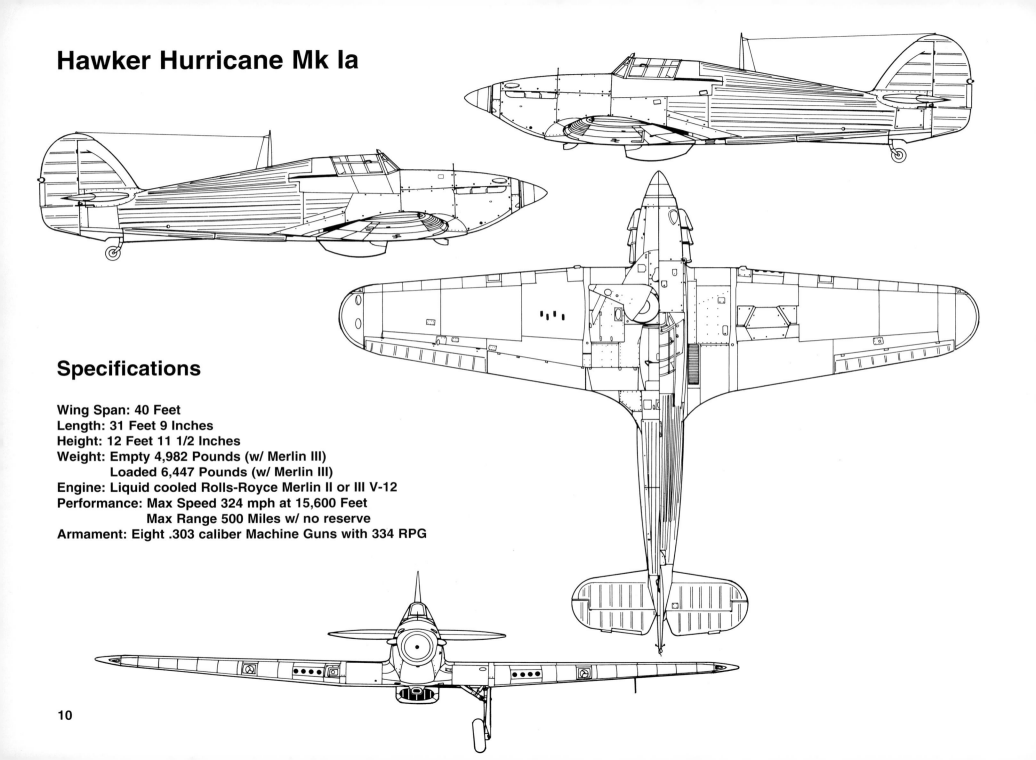

Hawker Hurricane Mk Ia

Specifications

Wing Span: 40 Feet
Length: 31 Feet 9 Inches
Height: 12 Feet 11 1/2 Inches
Weight: Empty 4,982 Pounds (w/ Merlin III)
　　　　　Loaded 6,447 Pounds (w/ Merlin III)
Engine: Liquid cooled Rolls-Royce Merlin II or III V-12
Performance: Max Speed 324 mph at 15,600 Feet
　　　　　　　Max Range 500 Miles w/ no reserve
Armament: Eight .303 caliber Machine Guns with 334 RPG

The pilot of a Middle East based Hurricane prepares to board his aircraft. This is a very early model with the original pattern windshield and ring-and-bead gun sight. The gun bay covers are the original cross-shaped pattern. The two louvers above the wing root vent hot air from the radiator compartment and cockpit and are on both sides of fuselage. The louvers were a common feature on tropicalized Hurricanes.

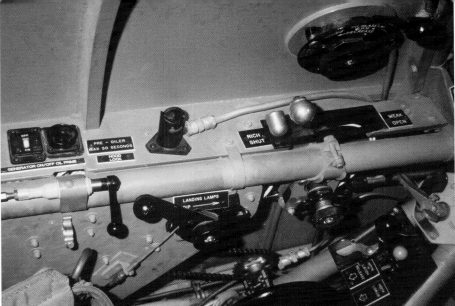

The tubular interior structure and a sheet metal panel supported the silver throttle and propeller pitch controls. The throttle friction adjustment wheel was immediately below the throttle. Immediately aft of the friction adjustment wheel is the black lever and cable which controls the angle of the landing lights. The Hurricane lacked built-up sidewalls or consoles in the cockpit.

The propeller revolution control unit is located above the main throttle levers. The brass bell switch in front of the throttle turns the landing lights on or off. The Sea Hurricane's arresting hook controls are mounted just below the red fuel-selector switch and its indicator dial. Separate levers lower the hook (right) and release it from the arresting wires (left). Aside from these controls, the cockpit layout changed little over the course of the Hurricane's life.

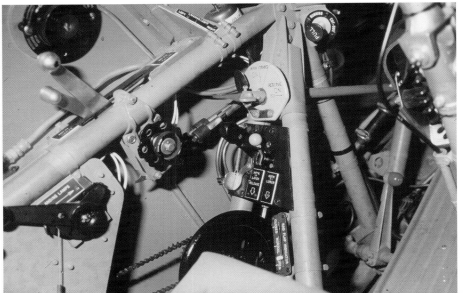

The control column has a black Bakelite spade-shaped hand grip with a brass-colored gun button on the upper left. The lever in the center of the grip operates the pneumatic brakes. All Hurricanes had an open floor.

(Above) The red lever at lower left is the control for switching between the main and reserve fuel tanks. On the starboard side of the instrument panel is the orange oil pressure gauge and the red fuel pressure gauge. Above these is the red rimmed boost gauge.

(Below) The compass was mounted horizontally on the lower frame of the instrument panel in front of the control column. The large star-shaped handle below the compass binnacle controls the fore and aft adjustment of the rudder bar. The brass plunger to the right of the compass is the Ki-Gass priming-pump for starting the engine. The control stick was hinged at its midpoint to provide aileron control.

The foot boards leading to the rudder pedals are angled outwards. The pedals were equipped with toe loops to keep the pilot's feet on the pedals during maneuvers. The black panel just above the right edge of pilot's seat is the flap and landing gear selector unit. The Hurricane's cockpit was painted Interior Grey-Green, while most of the add-on fittings were black.

Originally the lower edge of the windshield fit flush with the fuselage. After the introduction of armor glass to the windshield, the lower edge of the frame became vertical. A liquid de-icing pipe runs along the lower edge of the windshield frame. A tank holding four pints of de-icer was located in the lower right section of the cockpit. The de-icing liquid is pumped using either a KI-GAS or Rotax unit.

The standard windshield frame from the later Mk I production batches onward consisted of two metal arches raked aft and connected by horizontal strips. The rearmost arch was braced with a tubular support. A bullet proof windshield was fitted into the forward arch. A rearview mirror was usually fitted to the top of the windscreen.

The Hurricane was originally fitted with a simple ring-and-bead gun sight. The reflector gun sight fits into a cut-out in the instrument panel and shroud. The sighting glass is supported by two angled 'U' brackets extending back onto the base of the sight.

The gun sight is mounted in a circular bracket whose support rods extend down at an angle to the instrument panel cross-tube. The sight was equipped with a shock absorbing 'sorbo-pad' for the pilot's protection.

To the right of the landing gear/flap panel is the FLIGHT/GROUND lever. It is switched to GROUND when using a Ground Starter Trolley and to FLIGHT when using the aircraft battery for engine start-up. The flap position indicator is below the landing gear/flap panel. It shows the range of flap operation between zero and eighty degrees in ten degree increments. To the right of the flap indicator is a brass plunger which operates the windscreen de-icing system. The silver 'T' handle operates the emergency flare.

A single lever operated the landing gear and flaps. The left side of the H pattern operated the landing gear while the right side operated the flaps. The lever was normally in the neutral position and only moved to actually operate the landing gear or flaps. The metal shape on the left is a flexible 'stop' which prevents accidentally raising the landing gear when the aircraft is on the ground.

Windscreens, Canopies, and Mirrors

Second Prototype and Early Production

Early Production with External Armor

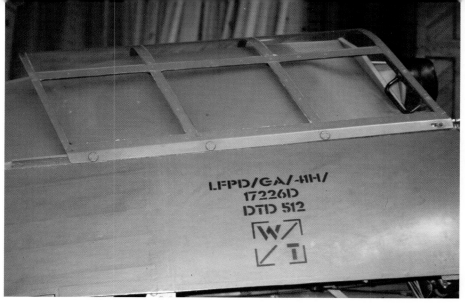

The Hurricane canopy frame consists of two angled metal strips, four inverted U-shaped frames, and two interim supports acting as additional stiffeners. The canopy slides to the rear on U-shaped tracks and can be jettisoned in flight. The interiors of the windscreen and canopy frames were usually painted matte black.

Late Production with Internal Armor

Mirror Types

The pilot's head is protected by armor plate secured to the top of the cockpit bulkhead. The pilot's shoulder harness strap bracket is fixed in its slot. The red fire extinguisher is modern equipment required for flying under Civil Aviation Authority (CAA) regulations. Land-based Hurricanes were not usually fitted with a headrest as provided on this Sea Hurricane.

17

(Above) A head rest was a necessary feature on Sea Hurricanes to cushion the shock effect of acceleration and deceleration when operating from Catapult Armed Merchantmen (CAM) ship launching ramps or carrier decks. The circular pad is mounted on a triangular metal frame fitted to the pilot's head armor plate.

(Above Left) The support frame for the rear view mirror is attached to the top of the windshield by screws. Brass hexagonal nuts retain the mirror in place on either side of the frame. This was the most common style of rearview mirror. Others included round and wedged-shaped styles.

(Left) Hurricane canopies have a knockout panel located in the port front panel to assist vision should the windshield be obscured for any reason. The pilot pushed a sliding plate along the top edge of the panel and pushed the panel outward.

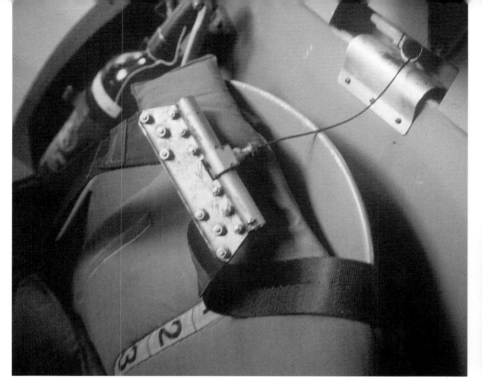

(Above) The pilot's shoulder harness straps are attached to a flexible wire which feeds back into a slot in the head armor. The harness attachment bracket is in its released position. The wire is normally held under tension by a spring and encased in a metal tube.

(Above Right) A black lever on the right cockpit frame releases the harness bracket should the pilot need to lean forward. The bracket is normally held in its slot when the pilot is flying the aircraft.

(Right) An emergency exit panel was fitted on the starboard side of the cockpit. To jettison the panel, the canopy had to be fully open. This action disengaged a bolt linked to the upper rear corner of the panel. The red lever was then pulled up and back, disengaging two retaining pins at the panel ends, allowing the pilot to complete the procedure by pushing out on the top edge of the panel. Although the panel could be removed to provide easier access for the groundcrew, it was rarely used for normal ingress and egress by the pilot.

The tapered radio mast supports an antenna wire which is channeled up from the fuse-lage. The mast extends down through the upper fuselage and is attached to a cross-member of the Warren Truss fuselage frame. Early Mk I Hurricanes carried untapered radio masts.

The aerial wire extends back from the radio mast to the rudder where it is attached to a small mast on the rudder post. The yellow fin marking above and in front of the fin flash denotes the Sea Hurricane's operations with the PEDESTAL convoy to Malta in August of 1942.

Antenna Masts

Untapered Mast   **Tapered Mast**

The antenna wire ends at a porcelain insulation cup. The cup is attached to the rudder post with a bolt passed through a wire loop. The wire loop is spring loaded to keep the antenna taut.

Rudder Antenna Post

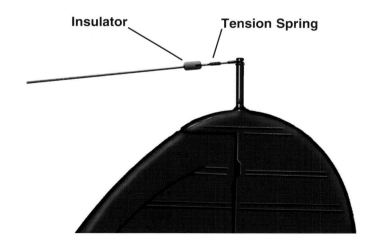

Insulator   Tension Spring

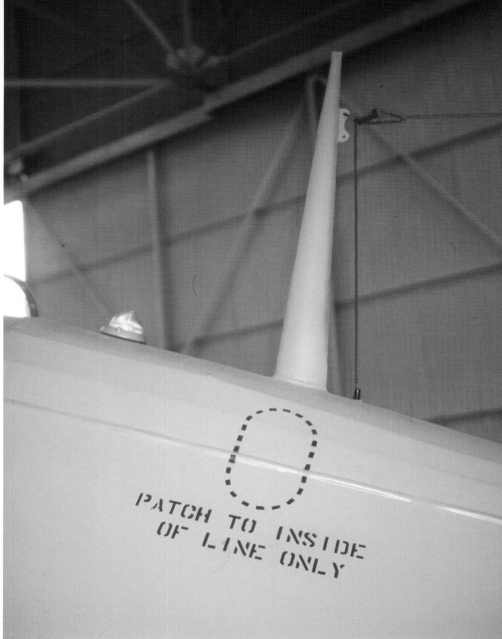

Hurricanes are fitted with an upward firing identification flare launcher. The launcher is located on the port fuselage side next to the radio mast. The upper identification light is located in front of the radio mast. Hurricane's using later radio systems dispensed with the antenna wires.

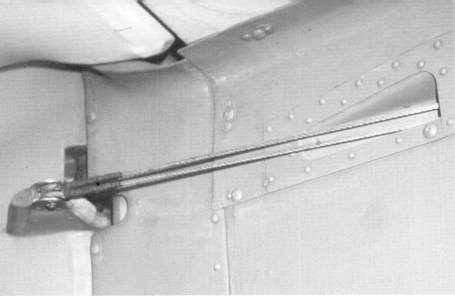

The rudder cables are fed into the lower tailplane fairing via a shallow channel plate secured to the fairing. Later Hurricanes from the Mk II onward featured plates with external covers.

The rear identification light is located above the trim tab. The light holder is secured to the rudder by small screws. The light was white.

The rudder hinge line on Hurricanes runs vertically to the top of the vertical stabilizer before angling forward. The upper front portion of the rudder encompasses a counter-balance weight. The vertical fin and rudder were offset 1.5 degrees to the left to counter engine and propeller torque.

The Hurricane's elevators consist of a metal frame with seven ribs. The frame is covered entirely by fabric stiffened with dope. Three hinges attached the elevator to the stabilizer. The elevators were equipped with both cockpit controlled and fixed trim tabs.

The inner edge of the elevator frame angles outward to provide clearance for the rudder and is rounded at the point where it meets with the flexible trim-tab. A fairing surrounds the torque tube connecting both elevators at the point of entry into the fuselage.

In contrast to all subsequent Marks, the Mk I Hurricane is fitted with a Servo trim tab on the rudder which automatically acted as a counter to the direction in which the rudder is moved. The tab's control wires are housed within the rudder.

In addition to flexible trim-tabs, the Hurricane's elevators have fixed tabs angled at five degrees. Their purpose is two-fold: one serving to counter-act the inherent tail-heaviness of the Hurricane and second, to lessen the stick forces necessary to maintain the proper flight attitude.

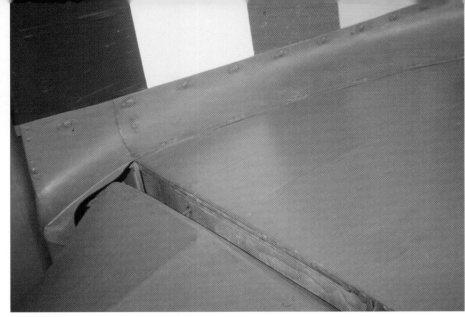

A fairing strip runs the full fore and aft length of the horizontal and vertical stabilizers and is attached to both with machine screws. Removal of the strip gains access to the vertical stabilizer attachment brackets.

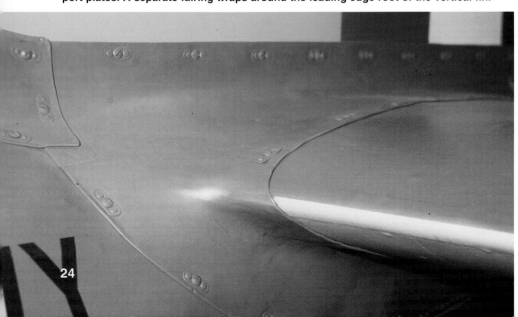

The fairing wraps around both the upper and lower surfaces of the horizontal stabilizer as well as the vertical fin. Each of the fairing's mounting screws have their own riveted support plates. A separate fairing wraps around the leading edge root of the vertical fin.

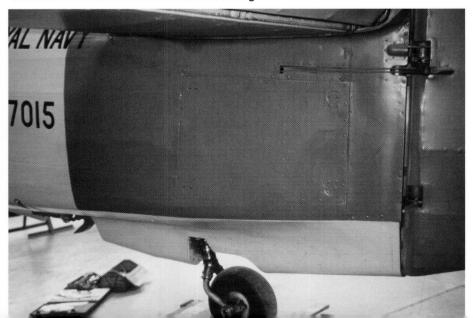

A rectangular metal panel provides access to the tail wheel assembly. The panel is held in place by quarter-turn fasteners at each corner. The exposed rudder cables slot into a channel in the rear of the lower stabilizer fairing.

A port side inspection panel in the Hurricane's rear fuselage provides access to the tail wheel support structure. The Interior Grey-Green fin post is anchored to this structure as well. The rudder cable channel is riveted to the lower horizontal stabilizer fairing. Early Hurricanes left the factory with the Warren truss fuselage structure painted silver. Later Hurricanes had them painted Interior Grey-Green. The red-doped fabric is stretched over varnished wood frames and stringers.

The ventral fairing under the aft fuselage was introduced during the initial production run of the Hurricane Mk I. The fairing improved the Hurricane's low speed lateral control and its ability to recover from a spin.

A cut out in the ventral fairing accommodates the tail wheel. The unit was originally retractable, but was fixed after a short period. Early production aircraft featured a simple spring shock absorber and lacked a link. In WW II the rectangular brackets at the end of the wheel fork accommodated the inverted U-shaped hooks of the manually operated tow and ground handling bars. The current towing unit is secured to the wheel hub.

This is the Dowty version introduced on the Mk II onwards. It featured an oleo-pneumatic shock absorber. The Lockheed Company also supplied similar tail wheel units for the Hurricane. The wheel is fully castoring as well as self-centering. The tail wheel yoke is an inverted 'U' with a rear support strip feeding up into the upper support column. The smooth treaded tire is produced by Dunlop and is self-grounding.

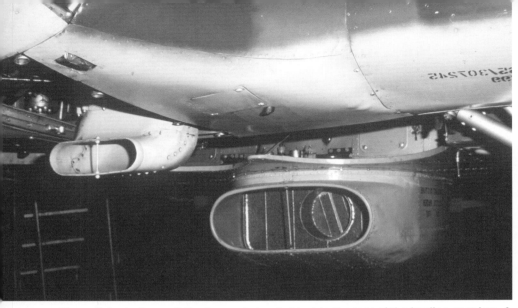

The radiator bath on all Hurricanes is located just to the rear of the landing gear bay. A stencil on the port side states the recommended coolant mixture is 70% water and 30% glycol. This is the later, and most common radiator with the circular oil cooler. The small scoop in the foreground is the carburetor air-intake.

Looking into the radiator bath from the rear, two fixed rods support the extreme end of the bath. Directly behind the radiator are the exit flap actuating rods. A cockpit lever with a thumb release button operates the flap and controls the velocity and volume of cooling air through the radiator. The circular aperture is the back end of the oil cooler.

This radiator is equipped with the early style rectangular oil cooler in the center of the assembly. A small vertical brace supports the lip of the fixed intake.

The rear end of the early style radiator is virtually identical to the later style with the circular oil cooler. The small panel in the roof of the radiator bath provides access to the oil cooler and radiator pipe couplings. It is hinged at the front and is secured by three quarter-turn fasteners.

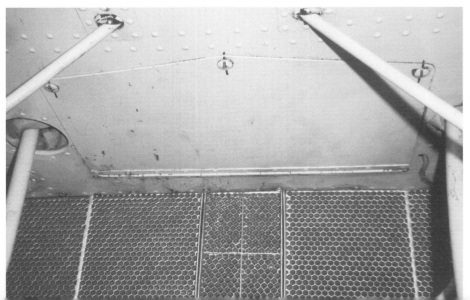

The cover of the radiator could be removed as a single unit. The radiator unit fits directly behind the front sealing strip which joins onto the rounded forward section of the cover. The cover is attached to the fuselage using machine screws through the flange on the upper edge of the cover.

The pneumatic system air bottle is mounted in the front center of the wheel bay. The air bottle is fed from an engine driven compressor located on the starboard rear end of the engine block. Maximum pressure is 300 lbs per square inch. The port and starboard wheel wells are one continuous unit with no central separation.

The stencil on the port side of the radiator cover details the correct mix of water and glycol for use in the aircraft's engine cooling system.

A small perspex window in the wheel well of the Hurricane allows the pilot to check the state of his landing gear. The small spring clip just visible above the rim of the wheel well is one of the mounts for securing the engine's crank handles.

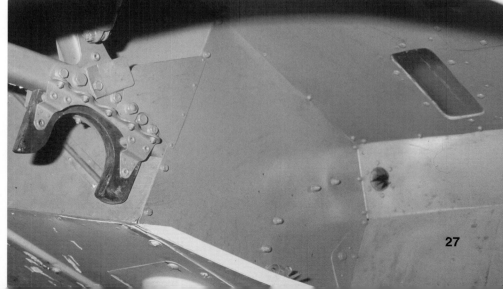

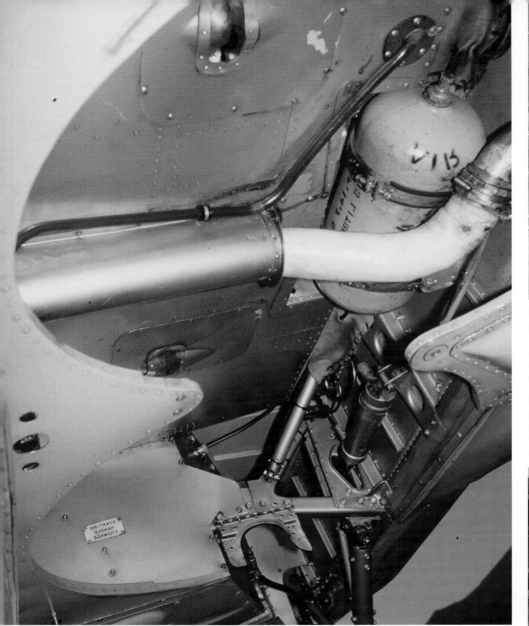

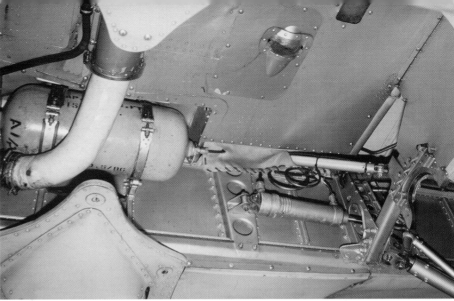

The roof of the wheel bay was smooth metal, broken only by a small sighting window and a catch for a 'stirrup' mounted on the wheel hub. The window allowed the pilot to check the status of the landing gear. The catch was engaged when the gear was retracted and the 'stirrup' on the wheel hub activated a switch for the cockpit landing gear position indicator. The wheel and strut bays of early Hurricanes were painted silver at the factory. Later aircraft had them painted Interior Grey-Green. (Enzio Maio)

The rear support strut for the landing gear fits into a bracket on the main strut. It acts as a radius rod and has an elbow joint towards the rear which flexes upon retraction, pulling the gear back through 7 degrees to fit into the wheel bay. The black braided pipe at the top of the main gear is part of the wheel braking system. The retraction and support struts were usually painted silver.

The Hurricane's brakes and guns were operated pneumatically. An engine driven compressor supplied air to a pressure cylinder mounted behind the front wing spar. The large pipe carries coolant between the engine and the radiator. The upside down, U-shaped bracket supports the landing gear's main strut. The entire landing gear bay, from the port landing gear strut to the starboard strut, was open which allowed easy access for the groundcrew. (Enzio Maio)

The wheel has a concave hub. The yellow fitting in the center is a 'stirrup' which engages an automatic catch in roof of the gear-bay. When fully engaged, a microswitch activates a red lamp on the gear position indicator located on the port side of the cockpit. The yellow cap covers the tire's air valve.

The absence of the wing fuel tank exposes the complete longitudinal support rod for the landing gear. The elbow joint for the landing gear radius rod splits to allow the support rod to pass through it.

The main landing gear cover extends down as far as the wheel hub. The cover is held on to the strut with constricting metal bands which wrap around the strut and are tightened with bolts. The remainder of the tire is uncovered when the gear is in the retracted position. The narrow tubing channels air to the Dunlop braking system. The system used small air-bags within the hubs to brake the wheels. The landing gear struts left the factory in a natural, anodized metal color. The landing gear strut was usually an anodized natural metal color. The interior of the strut cover was silver.

Metal bands hold the cover to the strut. The landing gear's support and retraction struts were usually painted silver at the factory. The inner faces of the landing gear covers were also painted silver.

The silver cylinder is the starboard landing gear hydraulic retraction jack. Coiled copper piping is fitted at either end of the unit. The inner end of the jack is mounted on a triangular bracket and secured by nuts. The gear support bracket is braced by a strut angled upward and secured to the upper facing of the wheel well.

The main landing gear cover consists of a single outer sheet of duralumin riveted to one main and two secondary inner pieces of flanged sheet. The assembly was bolted to four brackets on the strut. The separate radius rod cover is held on by two bolted brackets.

The rear support strut is housed within its own well. It is angled to allow for the seven degree backward movement of the landing gear.

The main fuel feed is located in the aft center of the wheel bay. The horizontal copper pipes link the wing fuel tanks while the vertical copper pipe leads to the fuselage header tank. The nuts securing the radiator cover to the underside of the wing can be seen under the outer rim of the cover.

All but the first few Hurricane wings were metal-skinned. The leading and trailing edges are parallel on the center sections, while the outer panels are tapered. Flush rivets are used only on the wing leading edge panels.

The outer wing panel's joint to the center panel is covered by a fairing on the top and bottom of the wing. The majority of the wing skins are fastened with mushroom headed rivets.

The outer wing sections are joined to the center section by four attachment points mounted in pairs on the front and rear wing spars. A circular male lug on the outer wing slots between two similar female fittings on the wing center section. The lugs are then secured with bolted pinions. These are the rear lugs and they slot in horizontally. The front lugs slot in vertically.

Mk I Fabric Wings

Mk IA Metal Wings

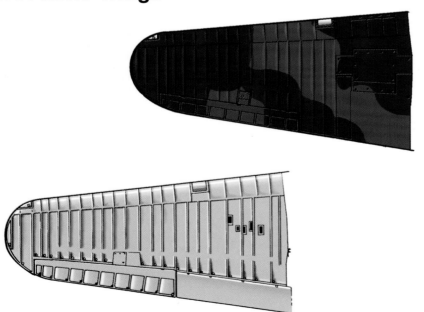

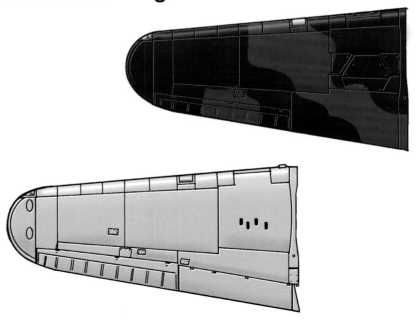

Two fuel tanks were housed in bays in the wing center section — one on each side of the fuselage. Each tank has a capacity of 34.5 gallons and is pressurized above 20,000 feet. Pressure was provided by the exhaust side of the vacuum pump. A pressurizing cock below the throttle quadrant is turned from 'ATMOSPHERE' to 'PRESSURE' whenever the fuel pressure warning light comes on. The vertical panel angling back at the front of the bay forms the rear wall of the wheel bay.

The left main fuel tank in position. Screws placed through lugs at each corner of the tank secure the unit to the wing frame. The two rows of Simmonds nuts used to secure the wing panel in position stand out against the tank's green color.

Mk IB Metal Wings

Mk IIC Metal Wings

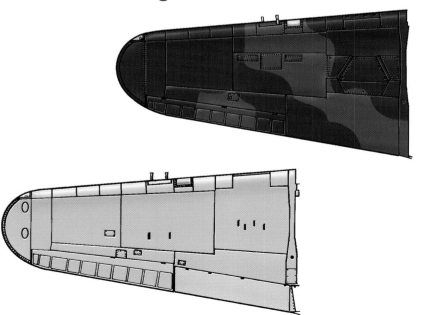

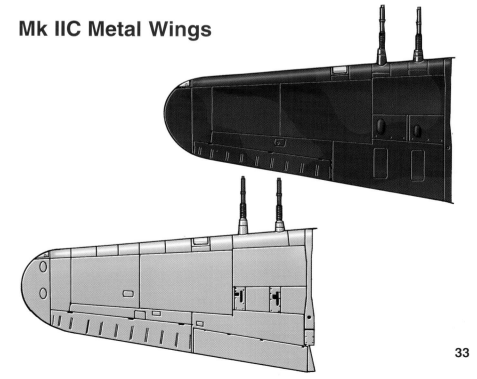

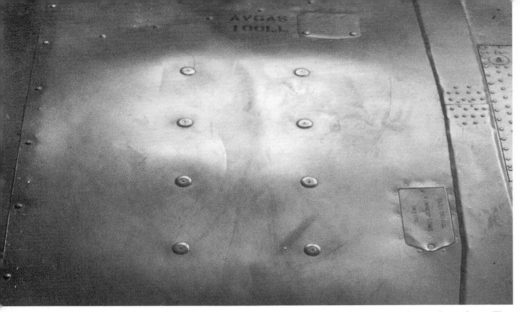

Two parallel rows of Simmonds nuts attach the wing tank cover to the tank surface. The metal cover is sufficiently strong to allow groundcrew to walk on it. The fuel filler cover is at the upper right and is marked with a stenciled reference to the type and quantity of fuel to be used. An electrical connections panel is located at the lower right of the panel next to the wing join faring.

Several removable panels on the fuselage side allowed access to the fuselage interior. The front panel provides maintenance access to the cockpit. The middle panel is the cover for the aircraft transmitter/receiver, with different variants being used by RAF and RN aircraft. The rear panel provided access to the fuselage. The cockpit cover and flying controls locking gear are also stowed here.

The main gun bay panel is denoted by the hexagonal outline. The two panels in line with the front of the main panel allow access to the ammunition containers. The gun bay cover on the original fabric wings had been in the shape of a cross. The gunbays were usually painted Interior Grey-Green.

Hurricane Mk IIC (LF738) is preserved at RAF Cosford. The bulges in the upper wing surface provide clearance for the cannon's cylindrical ammunition drums. The rectangular covers in the foreground provide access to the cannon breeches.

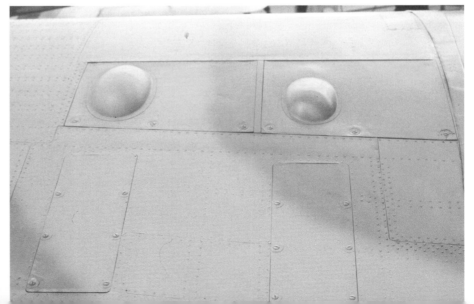

The L-shaped pitot mast was suspended from the port wing. The end of the pitot tube was electrically heated which left it a light metallic brown color. The red tape on the pitot cover is a reminder to the groundcrew to remove it when preparing the aircraft for flight.

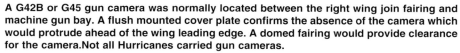

A G42B or G45 gun camera was normally located between the right wing join fairing and machine gun bay. A flush mounted cover plate confirms the absence of the camera which would protrude ahead of the wing leading edge. A domed fairing would provide clearance for the camera.Not all Hurricanes carried gun cameras.

Navigation lights are mounted on each wing tip — a red bulb on the port wing and a blue-green bulb on the starboard wing — both under clear covers. The wing tips are detachable along a line running from the aileron to the navigation light. The two oval inspection panels provide access to the wing tip's eight securing bolts.

The square stencil with 'W/T' inside is one of several applied at different points on the aircraft (fin, rudder, the fuselage above the radio hatch and the wing-tip underside, as seen here). The stencils refer to the flight control surfaces which have to be bonded with the airframe to prevent a static electric build-up from (for example) the movement of coolant or fuel in the pipes or the aircraft's own motion. Proper bonding action ensures enhanced radio transmission and reception.

The leading edge of the Mk XIIB Hurricane wing reveals both the basic four gun layout of the 'A' wing and the two additional guns used on the 'B' wing. The latter pair are staggered vertically and horizontally to provide clearance for the ammunition feed chutes in the thinner outer wing section. The red doped covers on the gun muzzles were used to keep dirt out of the weapons.

The landing lamps are housed in square frames and located in the middle of each wing leading edge. They are mounted on gimbals to permit them to be dipped using a control lever in the cockpit.

The landing light locations in the center leading edge of each wing are another standard Hurricane feature. The light windows are made of acetate sheet and are secured to a frame positioned between two nose ribs.

Spent machine gun cartridge cases were ejected through slots in the underside of the wing. The cases are ejected on the opposite side of the magazine feeds and are channeled down through metal chutes bolted to plates attached to the inside of the lower wing skin. Felt pads are fitted where the chutes link up with the guns. The V- pattern rivets enclosing the slots follow the lines of the Warren truss framework within the wing spars.

Hurricane landing flaps consist of two sections on each wing — a single flap in the wing center section and another flap on the wing's outer panel. Rib inserts provided structural rigidity. The center section flaps are joined together with a single torque tube passing above the radiator bath. A universal joint connects the center section flap to the outer section flap. A hydraulic jack positioned inside the port flap operates all four flap sections.

The center section flap has two hinges, while the outer sections have four hinges. This pair are on either side of the fairing covering the gap between the inner and outer flap sections.

A spring loaded triangular plate located directly below the wing join fairing closes the gap between the center and outer flap sections. The flaps can be manually raised and lowered using a lever positioned on the starboard side of the pilot's seat.

A nine gallon oil tank is mounted inside the leading edge of the port wing center section. The filler cap is fitted on the outer edge. An additional access panel is located on the lower inner side of the tank. The tank is permanently pressurized at four P.S.I. to prevent aeration of the oil. Pressure is maintained by a control valve located forward of the firewall on the starboard side.

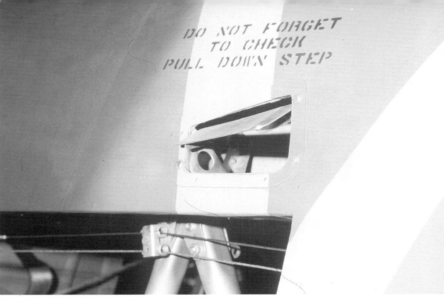

The port side of the Sea Hurricane with all the side panels in position shows the standard means of access to the cockpit. The First Aid kit was normally housed in the lower left section of the panel directly behind the kick-in step. Although not shown here, a dotted square "break-in" outline was usually painted on the panel to mark the kit's location. The turn-over pylon struts are housed in the upper fuselage immediately behind the cockpit.

With his right foot in the stirrup, the pilot reaches up with his right hand for the hand insert which has a hinged cover. When up on the wing, a push on the hand grip releases the lock on the stirrup and a bungee cord pulls it back into its socket. The warning stenciled on the fuselage refers to the procedure for getting down from the aircraft. The foot rest has to be pulled down by ground personnel, otherwise the pilot had to jump down from the wing. The wires run between the trim controls in the cockpit and the trim tabs on the empennage.

Entry into the Hurricane cockpit is made on the port side in three stages. The first stage involves the retractable foot stirrup which is pulled down into position. Operation of the foot-rest automatically opens the hand insert on the fuselage side.

Once up on the wing, the pilot uses this spring loaded kick step to climb into the cockpit. A very prominent reminder about turning on the oxygen supply is stenciled on the fuselage.

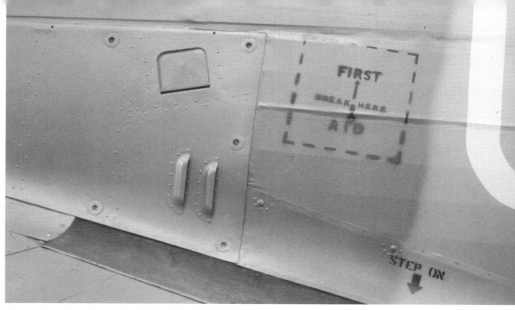

The Emergency Landing Flare on the Sea Hurricane is mounted in a cylindrical chute on the port side of the fuselage behind a removable panel. The fuselage access panel securing mounts can be seen attached to the Warren Truss tubular fuselage frames. The panel securing screws have two pins on the end. The screw pins are pushed vertically through the gap in the center of the mount and locked into position when they are turned through 90 degrees.

A red stencil on the port side hatch of LF738 indicates the location of the Hurricane's First Aid kit. The twin louvers above the walk-way drew hot air out of the cockpit — particularly useful when the aircraft operated in tropical climates.

The underside of the Sea Hurricane reveals the cover for the Emergency Landing Flare with the "Free/Locked" lever alongside. A cockpit control unlocked the cover with the weight of the flare doing the rest. The cover could not be closed in flight. The downward identification light is located on the fuselage center line.

The open radio compartment immediately aft of the cockpit would normally house a TR9D, TR1133B, or D set on RAF aircraft. The latter installation dispensed with an external aerial wire. The mast alone acted as an aerial and had a cable connecting it to the radio set.

The silver colored compressor air control unit is mounted on the upper starboard quarter of the engine firewall. The unit vents air through the valve at the top when the pressure exceeds 300 P.S.I. The bowl underneath the unit collects residue which could foul the unit. Behind the firewall is the 28 gallon reserve fuel tank.

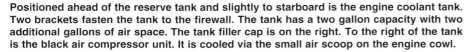

Positioned ahead of the reserve tank and slightly to starboard is the engine coolant tank. Two brackets fasten the tank to the firewall. The tank has a two gallon capacity with two additional gallons of air space. The tank filler cap is on the right. To the right of the tank is the black air compressor unit. It is cooled via the small air scoop on the engine cowl.

The engine bearers were bolted and riveted together. Secondary support tubes were welded in place. The riveted reinforcing plate at the intersection of the engine bearers supported the right rear engine mount. The green box houses the oil/air separator which is operated by the pressure side of the vacuum pump. Air is ejected from the top while oil is channeled out via the pipe at the base of the separator. The silver toothed wheel is the central gear bearing for the manual engine starter. The entire engine bay has been sprayed Interior Grey-Green.

The toothed wheels and chains form part of the engine's manual starting system. A crank handle is inserted in the aperture in the forwardmost wheel. A second aperture is on the opposite side of the engine. The crank handles are stored in the wheel wells.

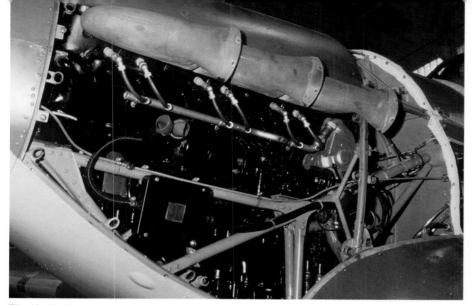

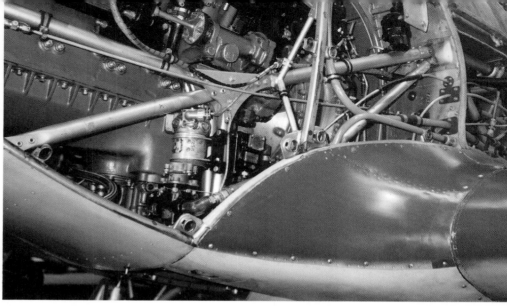

The Merlin III engine was fitted to late Mk I Hurricanes. The front and rear engine mounts are strengthened by angular reinforcements on the engine bearers. The bearers are painted Interior Grey-Green. The six spark plug leads are grouped in pairs under the three 'fish-tailed' exhaust manifolds.

The wing to fuselage joint was faired in with formed sheet metal. Some Hurricanes had a small air intake in the leading edge fairing.

The Merlin engine fitted to the Duxford Mk XIIB is a series 500. This was a post-war variant produced to the more stringent requirements of the civil aviation market. The fuselage panels from the engine's front cowl ring to the cockpit were removable for easy access for the ground crew.

The generator cooling ports protrude from the port side cowl panels. The circular aperture on the lower side is the socket for one of the two crank handles used for manually starting the engine. It is also the datum point from which to calculate the fore and aft limits of the aircraft's center of gravity (CG).

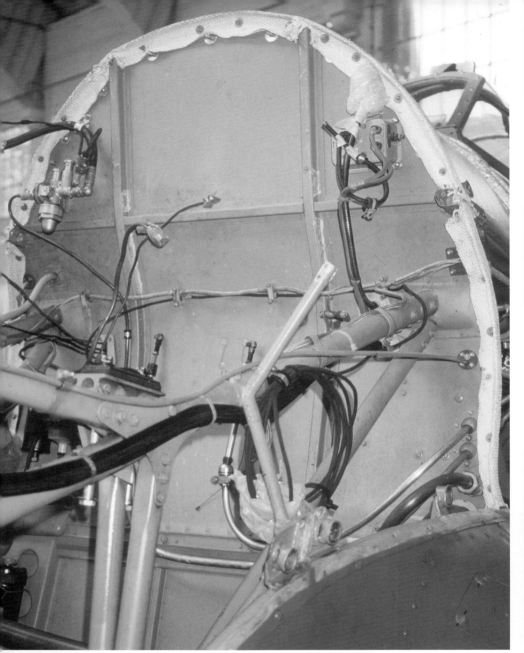

The removal of the engine reveals the firewall. The firewall, consisting of an asbestos sheet sandwiched between two duralumin panels, was mounted on the forward wing spar. The upper engine bearers are attached to the upper section of the firewall and the fuselage structure.

An early Hurricane Mk I of either No. 1 or No. 73 Sqdn is about to have its Merlin II or III engine brought to life by two airmen turning the crank handles inserted into the lower engine cowling. The airmen's' proximity to the propeller made this particular duty unpopular for obvious reasons! The aircraft is equipped with the original 'kidney' exhausts with their six slits. The engine cowling front appears to marginally over-lap the Watts spinner.

The Hurricane Mk I hanging in the Science Museum in London retains its early de Havilland three-bladed propeller and pointed spinner. Hurricane Mk Is were powered with a Rolls Royce Merlin II or III engine. The later Hurricane Mk II used the Merlin XX engine. The longer length of the engine lengthened the Hurricane's nose and slightly altered the contours of the cowl panels. (Enzio Maio)

'Fish-tail' exhaust pipes were introduced in place of the ejector exhaust manifolds. A small blister on the forward cowling provided clearance for the front of the engine.

Small bulges around the front cowl ring provide clearance for engine mounted accessories under the cowl. The small oblong hole under the nose permits checking of the timing plug and its locking wire.

Rotol propellers were introduced in late 1939 and had variable pitch blades and constant-speed units. Both features were vital in enhancing the Hurricane's performance to a level approaching that of its principal rival — the Messerschmitt Bf 109E. The oil collector channel, which wrapped around the top of the cowl just behind the spinner, is not fitted on this Hurricane.

43

The raised lip on the Hurricane's cowling front is the oil collector channel which was fitted to the final batch of Hawker-produced Mk Is. It prevented oil from seeping back over the cowl and fouling the windscreen. It is held in position by simple machine screws. Its use in squadron service appears to have been optional.

Exhausts

Prototype

Ejector

Kidney

Fishtail

The removal of the engine's forward cowl ring exposes the vacuum pump on the starboard side. The pump powers vacuum operated instruments on the instrument panel.

The Rotol propeller has a radius varying between 10 feet 9 inches and 11 feet 3 inches depending on the variant used. The blade pitch ranges from 23 to 53 degrees. The bulge in the lower cowling lip provides clearance for the vacuum pump which provides suction for vacuum operated instruments in the cockpit instrument panel.

Propellers

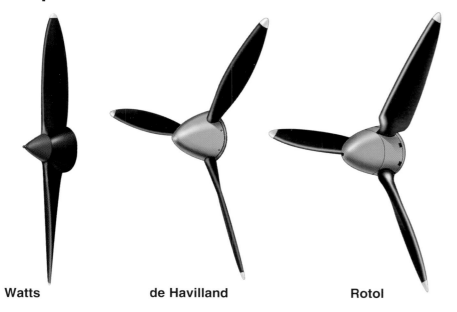

Watts   de Havilland   Rotol

The propeller constant speed unit is mounted on the port side of the engine opposite the vacuum pump. Both units are in front of the propeller reduction gear cover.

(Above) No. 3 Squadron soon followed 111 Squadron in converting to Hurricanes in March of 1938, but was soon forced to return to their Gladiator biplanes. This was due to the small size of Kenley airfield which brought about a series of landing accidents. Type B roundels are carried on the fuselage and upper port wing. The squadron code letter is applied around the aircraft serial. A Type B camouflage scheme of Dark Green and Dark Earth is applied over the upper surfaces. The Type B scheme was a simple reversal of the Type A scheme (see page 69).

(Below) Out with the old, and in with the new. A trio of Gloster Gauntlet biplane fighters lift off from North Weald while in the foreground stand three Hurricanes assigned to 56 Squadron. The Hurricanes are equipped with Watts two-bladed, fixed pitch, wooden propellers. The propellers were normally painted black.

Prior to W W II some Hurricane squadrons carried a broad arrow head design on the vertical fin. Some units painted the squadron badge on the arrow head. In this case 73 Squadron also applied their number to the fin. The Watts spinners were generally painted black with a light colored tip.

Servicing conditions during the Battle of France were basic as demonstrated by this party of 85 Sqdn armorers. The Hurricane is ready for action with the pilot's parachute pack placed on the port stabilizer, the foot-rest pulled down, and the harness straps laid out on cockpit rim. A starter battery is plugged in under the engine cowling. The yellow square on the port wing tip is a gas warning patch. The fuselage roundel bears a very thin yellow edge. The hexagon shape on the fin is a squadron Flight marking.

XR~T is a Canadian-built Hurricane Mk XIIB — equivalent to the British-built Mk IIB. The aircraft is painted in the colors and marking of No. 71 'Eagle' Squadron which was composed of US volunteers during 1940 through 1942. It performs regularly at air-shows. XR~T's spinner is not the correct shape for a Mk II having a more rounded tip. The aircraft has a 'B' wing with a total of 12 .303 caliber machine guns. The combination of fabric over the fuselage stringers and the sun's angle gives the impression of corrugated metal on the aft fuselage. (Enzio Maio)

The ailerons are slightly deflected as XR~T rolls to port. On a slow pass, the pilot's foot step is still hanging down. Normally it would have been retracted into its well. With the aircraft on all three landing gear, the flaps hang almost vertically. The wide track of the landing gear and low to medium pressure tires made taxiing the aircraft easier over rough fields. This was an especially attractive feature during the North African campaign where units moved from one unimproved airfield to another on a regular basis. The aircraft is taxied with the elevators in the 'up' position to prevent bursts of power from lifting the tail. (Enzio Maio)

This initial production Mk I was still fitted with the original fabric covered wings in 1940. On 18 August 1940 Pilot Officer Looker of 615 Sqdn brought the heavily damaged fighter into Croydon airfield, but not before he was fired upon by the AA defenses! The aircraft is photographed after the war fully restored and ready for entry into the Science Museum in London. The aircraft retains the original windshield with the curved base.

A pair of 46 Sqdn Hurricanes are being loaded for transfer to HMS *Glorious* from where they will be flown off to assist in the Norwegian Campaign. Several were landed back on *Glorious* when the Campaign ended despite the absence of any arresting gear or pilots' training in deck landings — a tragically vain act since the ship was sunk the next day by the German battlecruisers *Scharnhorst* and *Gneisenau* with heavy loss of life. The casualties included all but two of the RAF pilots. The Hurricane's undersides are black and white divided along the fuselage center line.

This initial production Mk I was assigned to 253 Sqdn. It crash landed on 1 May 1940, bending the De Havilland propeller in the process. The absence of gun muzzle tapes suggests that the aircraft was involved in combat. No fin flashes are applied although these were unofficially introduced several weeks prior to the incident. Type A fuselage roundels have been retained despite Type A1 replacements (adding a yellow ring) being introduced on the same date as the fin flashes.

Two Women's Royal Naval Service (WRNS) personnel load the ammunition magazines on a Mk 1B Hurricane. The rounds are fed into the feed chutes via rollers in the magazines. The holes in the front wing spar through which the gun barrels are inserted can be seen. The aircraft bears the standard naval camouflage scheme of Dark Slate Grey and Extra Dark Sea Grey upper surfaces over Medium Sea Grey under surfaces. A Type B roundel is on the upper wing surface, while a Type C.1 roundel is on the fuselage side.

The Sea Hurricane

(Right) This Sea Hurricane (Z7015) was originally a land-based Hurricane Mk I built in Canada. It was converted to the Sea Hurricane Mk I configuration in 1941. It was not airworthy for many years until it was purchased and restored by its Shuttleworth Trust owners. It is now on the airshow circuit over Britain. Z7015 is seen at the Spitfire Jubilee Display at Duxford in 1996.

(Below) Sea Hurricane's had a strengthened airframe, catapult spools, and an arresting hook, but were otherwise similar to their land-based counterparts. Sea Hurricanes were camouflaged in Extra Dark Sea Grey (a dark grey) and Dark Slate Grey (a grey with a distinctly greenish cast) upper surfaces over Medium Sea Grey under surfaces. The national markings were identical to those of the RAF. Z7015 also wears the yellow fin marking of the PEDESTAL convoy to Malta in 1942. The aircraft retains the original pattern exhausts which duct two cylinders into a single exhaust.

The merchant vessel Empire Lawrence was equipped with an angled launch-ramp. Ships so equipped were known as Catapult Armed Merchantmen (CAM) ships. The pilot's options after an action was completed were limited — either bale out over the convoy and be picked up, or head for the nearest friendly airfield if fuel supplies permitted.

(Above) Armorers service the weapons of a Sea Hurricane Mk IB. The gun camera protrudes from its detached aperture inboard of the starboard bank of machine guns. The radio-mast, aerial wire, and the upward identification light covers are also visible. The row of six screws ahead of the windshield provide attachment points for the starboard anti-glare shield.

(Below) The Shuttleworth Collection's Sea Hurricane is a short-nosed Mk I with the Merlin III engine and the longer spinner and Rotol propeller commonly seen on the later Hurricane Mk II. Beyond the modifications necessary for carrier operations, the Sea Hurricane Mk I was virtually identical to its land based counterpart in the RAF. The antenna hanging from the starboard wing roundel is a modern addition.

(Above) The Mk 1B Sea Hurricane was the first truly 'navalized' version, being fitted with a V-frame arresting hook under the rear fuselage. This fighter (AF962) is a Canadian-built Mk X powered by a Packard Merlin 28 engine and bearing a De Haviland propeller and exhaust glare shields. The latter is angled upwards, a feature of Canadian-produced fighters. The catapult point behind fuselage roundel has been capped.

The red wheels on either side of the Sea Hurricane's radiator bath are the catapult spools. These rest on the forward section of the launching-ramp sled. Compare the radiator's mesh screen pattern with that of the Hurricane Mk IIB on page 26.

The standard cover plates at the arresting hook's hinge points are curved to allow them to conform to the lower fuselage. The circular port is the aft attachment point for the catapult.

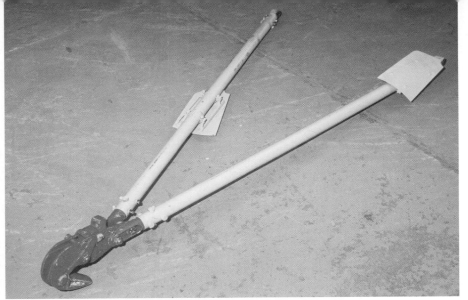

The arresting hook is a simple V-shaped fitting weighing 22 lbs. The open ends pivot from the lower fuselage frame. The pivots are covered by the attached rectangular plates. A hydraulic damper is attached to the port hinge point inside the fuselage. The damper controls the hook's downward motion and prevents the hook from bouncing off the deck and striking the fuselage during deck landings.

Sea Hurricane Arresting Hook

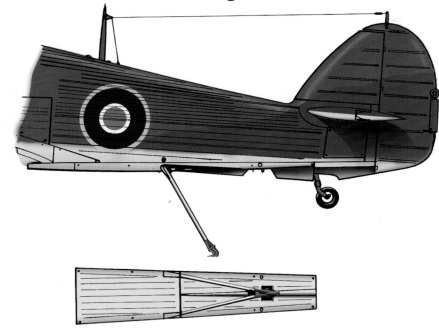

The arresting hook arms are slotted into channels on the underside of the fuselage. The standard cover plates are slightly wider than the hook arms and are hinged to accommodate the hook's movement. The silver plate over the hinge point is a temporary fitting and is not standard.

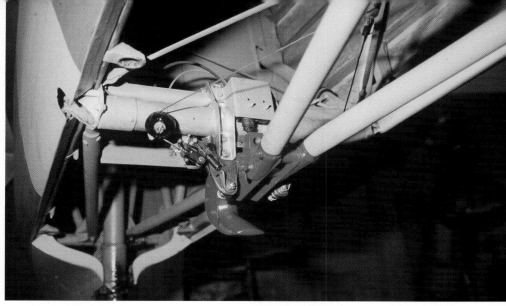

The arresting hook is held in the up position by twin latches which are bolted to an airframe cross member and the lifting bar socket. A hook release cable is routed to both sides of the latching gear via pulleys. A pair of levers on the port side of the cockpit releases the hook from the latches and disengages it from the arresting wire after landing.

The jaws of the arresting hook latch are barely visible with the ventral fairing cover in position. Just above the arresting hook's latches is the socket for the fuselage lifting bar.

A scoop on the leading edge of the port wing root acts as an air vent for the fuel filter unit located alongside the rear of the engine block.

P3428 was a Hawker produced Mk I. Judging by the absence of squadron codes and the white helmet worn by the pilot, the aircraft is believed to be on a company test flight. The aircraft is fitted with a Rotol constant-speed propeller. It served with 245 Sqdn until 'written-off' in a flying accident on 26 June 1941.

This Mk I Hurricane of 208 Sqdn is stripped of the engine center and rear fuselage panels as it undergoes a major inspection in the Western Desert. Proper servicing facilities were at a premium in this theater of operations. The aircraft was posted as 'missing' on 29 Jan 1941.

This Hurricane based in Oregon, USA bears the serial number of a Mk I which was Struck Off Charge (SOC) in May of 1940. In fact it is a Canadian-built Mk II which is camouflaged and marked in a typical Battle of Britain style. The inscription on the cowling is CHURCHILL'S CHICKS, although the correct expression was DOWDING'S CHICKS. Air Marshall Hugh Dowding was the head of RAF Fighter Command during the Battle of Britain.

This Mk I came from the final production run by Gloster during 1941 and, being attached to three different training units, never saw front line service. It bears the insignia of the Empire Central Flying School on the lower cowling. Hurricanes equipped with De Havilland propellers tended to be fitted with oil collector channels between the cowling and the spinner. The air flow around the fuselage and wing carries the exhaust stain aft and down towards the wingroot.

Armorers feed .303 caliber ammunition into a Hurricane's port wing ammunition magazines. The magazines were fitted in an upright position. The curved shapes attached to the forward end of the gun breeches are the ammunition feed chutes. The gun bay's hexagonal-shaped center cover appears to have been introduced on middle and late production Mk Is with metal wings. The airman on the right wears an Observer flying badge, probably earned during WW1.

Hawker Hurricane IIc

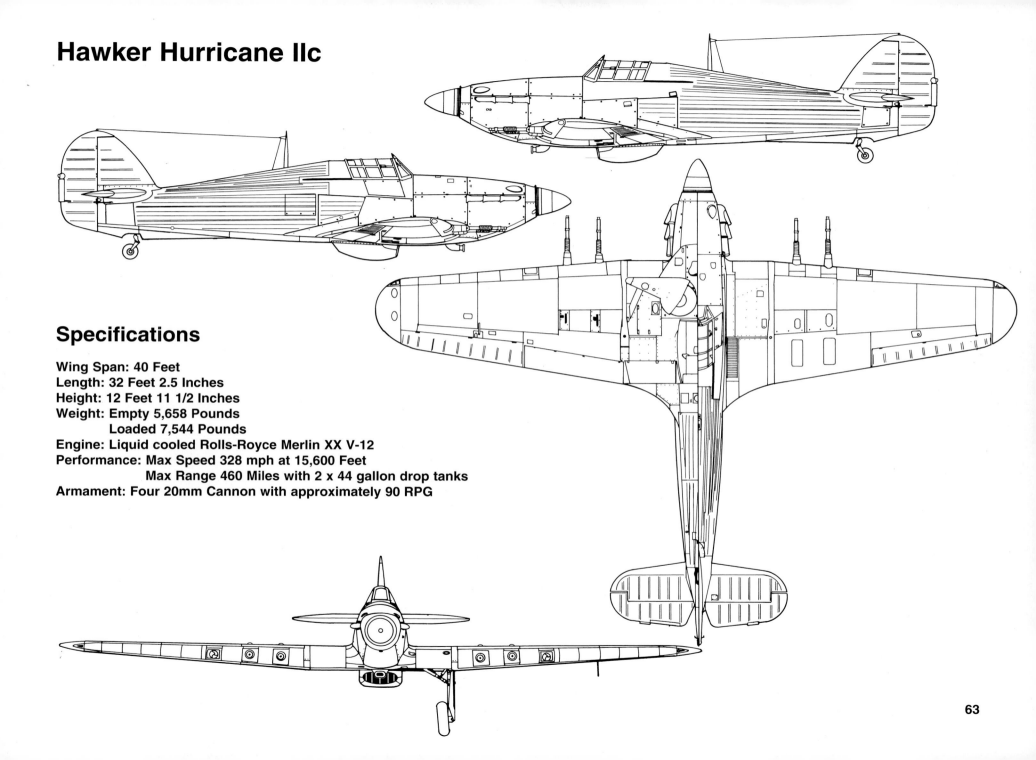

Specifications

Wing Span: 40 Feet
Length: 32 Feet 2.5 Inches
Height: 12 Feet 11 1/2 Inches
Weight: Empty 5,658 Pounds
       Loaded 7,544 Pounds
Engine: Liquid cooled Rolls-Royce Merlin XX V-12
Performance: Max Speed 328 mph at 15,600 Feet
       Max Range 460 Miles with 2 x 44 gallon drop tanks
Armament: Four 20mm Cannon with approximately 90 RPG

The current markings borne by PZ865 of the Battle of Britain Memorial Flight (BBMF) depict an aircraft based on Malta. The upper camouflage is Dark Earth and Mid Stone, while the under surfaces are split between Sky and black along the fuselage centerline. The cannon barrels are mockups.

The Hurricane Mk II introduced the Rolls-Royce Merlin XX engine which was slightly longer than the Merlin II and III used in the Hurricane Mk I. The additional engine length added about 10 inches to the nose of the aircraft. PZ865 is equipped with six non-standard multiple ejector exhausts.

(Below) Hurricane Mk IIDs in concert with a pair of Spitfire Mk Vs are seen somewhere in the Middle East around 1942/43. The camouflage is Dark Earth and Middle Stone upper surfaces over Azure Blue under surfaces. All spinners bear distinctive red paint. The recoil from firing the 'S' guns retarded the Hurricane Mk IID's already modest top speed of 254 mph by as much as 15 mph!

This 111 Sqdn Mk I came from the initial production batch and is under repair following a crash. The radiator cover lies in the right foreground while the radiator lies alongside wing join fairings. The radio compartment behind the cockpit is blocked off by fuselage stringers, but the reason for this is unknown. The aircraft was later reassigned to the Air Fighting Development Unit (APHID) and was finally Struck-Off-Charge in 1944.

The airframe structure of the Hurricane was only slightly removed from its predecessors of the late 1920s and early 1930s. Nevertheless, the Warren Truss metal frame, metal and wood formers, wood stringers in the fuselage — all covered in sheet metal panels and fabric — proved to be remarkably strong and damage resistant. Both Hurricanes have been stripped for parts, and possibly souvenirs, in this aircraft graveyard in Greece.

The Mk IID Hurricane was equipped with a pair of 40 mm Vickers 'S' guns mounted under each wing. A single .303 caliber machine gun was retained in each wing for sighting purposes. This is a preserved example of the 'S' gun at the RAF Museum, Hendon.

Vickers 40mm 'S' Gun

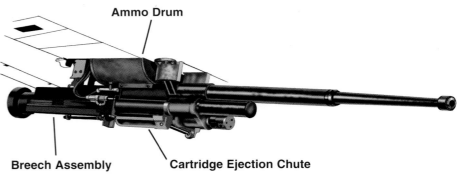

Ammo Drum

Breech Assembly   Cartridge Ejection Chute

The entire aft fuselage was made of wood formers and stringers built around the metal Warren truss frame. The aft fuselage was fabric covered. The fabric was given a red primer coat to shrink it, and then the camouflage colored dopes were applied. The tightly stretched fabric allows the fuselage stringers to stand out.

Camouflage Colors and Markings

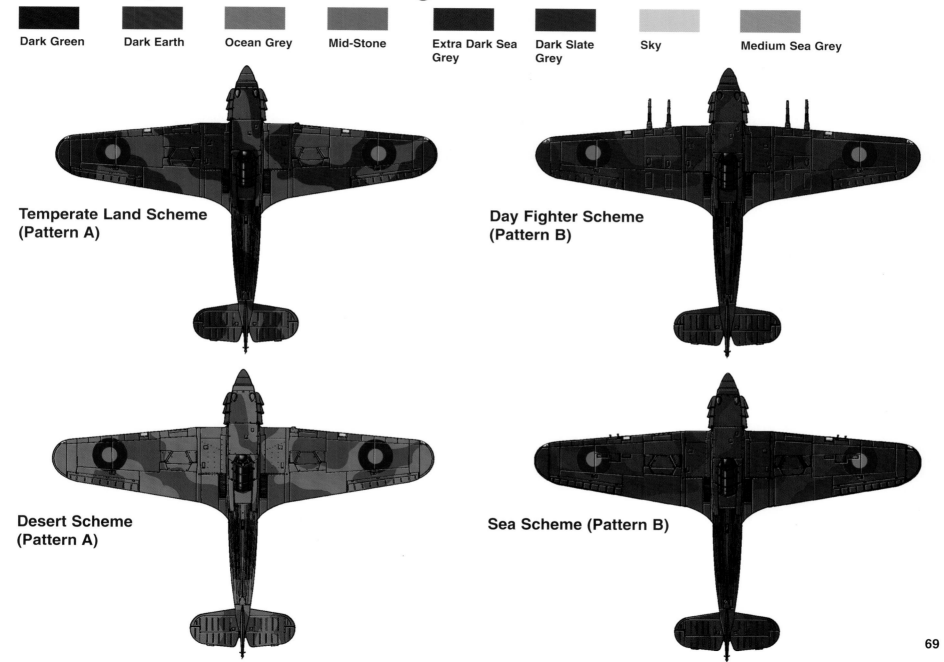

Dark Green   Dark Earth   Ocean Grey   Mid-Stone   Extra Dark Sea Grey   Dark Slate Grey   Sky   Medium Sea Grey

Temperate Land Scheme (Pattern A)

Day Fighter Scheme (Pattern B)

Desert Scheme (Pattern A)

Sea Scheme (Pattern B)

(Above) The Mk IV Hurricane embodied a true 'universal' wing that could mount different weapons or external stores without the need to alter the armament circuits or fuel systems. The prototype Mk IV (KX405) mounted a four-bladed Rotol propeller and a Merlin 32 engine, but KZ193 was more representative of the Mark IV with a three-bladed propeller and Merlin 27 engine. Mk IVs were equipped with additional engine and radiator armor. Many of the later Hurricanes optimized for the ground attack role were equipped with larger radiators to improve cooling at low altitudes.

(Below) The Hurricane Mk IID was a Mk IIA Series 2 variant specifically equipped with two underwing 40mm Vickers 'S' guns for use against armored ground targets. Although Rolls-Royce produced a prototype 12 round belt fed gun, it was the Vickers 'S' gun that was adopted. The gun was drum fed with a magazine capacity of 15 rounds. The wire extending from the fuselage to the stabilizer tips is for the Identification Friend or Foe (IFF) system.

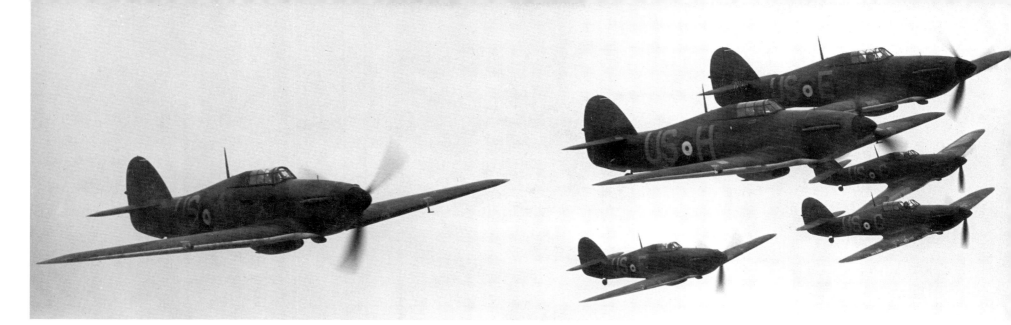

A close formation of 56 Sqdn Mk Is during late 1939 or early 1940. Black and white under surfaces can be seen on the majority of the aircraft. Type B upper wing roundels were added after November of 1939. Fin flashes would not be officially introduced until the spring of 1940.

(Below) NN~D (W9323) was a Gloster-built Hurricane Mk 1 assigned to the Squadron Leader of 310 (Czech) Squadron. The unit was based at Duxford during the Battle of Britain. The aircraft is camouflaged in the standard scheme of Dark Earth and Dark Green over Sky. The Rotol spinner and aft fuselage band are Sky, while the fuselage codes are Medium Sea Grey. An exhaust glare shield is mounted on the fuselage in front of the cockpit. 310 Squadron later transitioned into Spitfires during the fall of 1941. (via Ludvik Klimek)

This Mk I came from the initial Mk I production batch which lacked the ventral fairing around the tail wheel. It was re-assigned from 3 Sqdn to 73 Sqdn. The practice of carrying the squadron number on the fin was unusual.

Flying Officer Paul Richey flew an early fabric-winged Hurricane Mk I (L1679) when assigned to No.1 Sqdn in France in May of 1940. Richey shared a Do 215 and is believed to have downed a Do 17Z in this aircraft. 'Dear old George', as it was called by Richey, was shot up by strafing Do 17Zs on 14 May 1940 and written off.

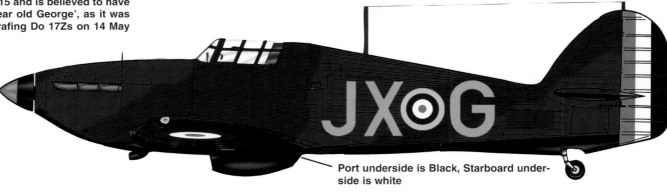

Port underside is Black, Starboard underside is white

Hurricane Mk I (White 22) was one of 20 Mk Is ordered by the Belgian Air Force. The airfcraft were equipped with fabric wings and Watts two-bladed wooden propellers. Most were destroyed on the ground during the initial German onslaught in May of 1940.

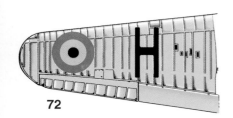

Silver doped undersurfaces

This Hurricane Mk IA flew with No. 615 Squadron in August of 1940 during the Battle of Britain. The aircraft is one of many Hurricane's fitted with a Spitfire propeller and spinner due to shortages of the de Havilland spinner and propeller normally used on the Hurricane.

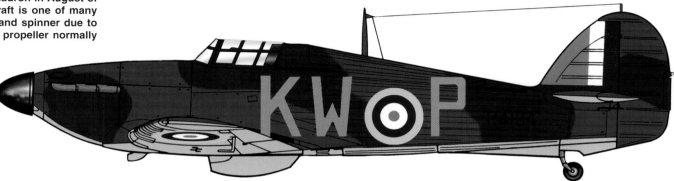

Hurricane Mk IIC (AK~G/BP592) flew with No. 213 Squadron in North Africa in 1942. Several RAF squadrons in North Africa experimented with partial mottled camouflage as used by the Axis Forces. The mottling was usually restricted to the nose and the leading edges of the wings. The pilot of this aircraft shot down three Luftwaffe Ju 88s over El Alamein on 1 September 1942 while flying this fighter.

Squadron Leader Smallwood flew a Hurricane Mk IIC (BE500) while commanding No. 87 Sqdn on nightfighter duties during 1940 and 1941. His blue and red command pennant was painted below the cockpit. The aircraft was overall Night Black.

UNITED PROVINCES
CAWNPORE 1

Wing Commander   Group Captain   Squadron Leader

The RAF's premier fighter Sqdn (No.1) operated Mk IIC Hurricanes between July of 1941 and September of 1942, after which it converted to the more advanced Hawker Typhoon. This photograph was taken just before the switch. All bear yellow identification stripes on their outboard wing leading edges and Sky fuselage bands.

The Last of the Many was the last Hurricane built. It was retained by Hawker for testing throughout the war and now flies at airshows in the UK. The 7 foot, 10 inch wide track of the Hurricane's landing gear made all aspects of ground handling easier and safer than that of the narrow tracked Supermarine Spitfire. This was especially true of aircraft carrier operations.

The Last of the Many makes a low pass at an airshow in the UK. The radiator exit flap has been opened to improve cooling when flying at moderate speeds at low altitude. The radiator was vulnerable to ground fire when the Hurricane was used in the close support role late in its career. Hurricane Mk IIDs and Mk IVs introduced an armored radiator housing which protected the radiator and oil cooler from damage and the often fatal loss of coolant. (Enzio Maio)

A Mk 1B Sea Hurricane of 885 Sqdn wears the colorful yellow recognition markings used when operating from *HMS Victorious* during the PEDESTAL convoy to Malta in August of 1942.

Hurricane Mk IIB (BE485) was assigned to No.402 Squadron for cross-channel attack operations. The unit was the second 'Hurribomber' squadron assigned to this role and began operations in late 1941. The standard armament was a pair of 250 lb bombs.

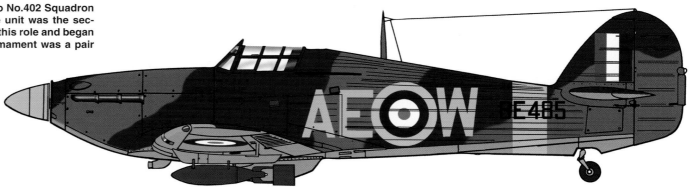

No 20 Sqdn (along with No. 5 Sqdn) operated the Hurricane Mk IID to good effect in Burma between 1943 and 1944. These aircraft were fitted with 40mm Vickers 'S' guns. Most of them were also fitted with tropical filters.

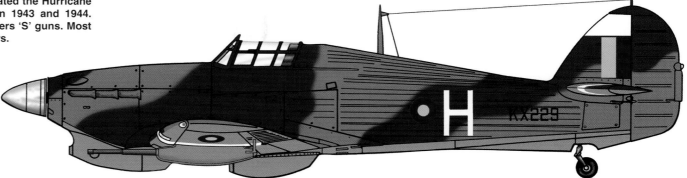

Hurricane IIC (LB935) flew as a reconnaissance aircraft assigned to No. 34 Squadron of the RAF's South East Asia Command in 1944. The Hurricanes were eventually replaced with US built P-47 Thunderbolts.

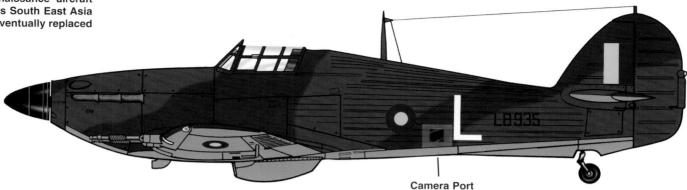

Camera Port

The Mk IV Hurricane was a heavily armored variant used for ground assault. This aircraft belonged to 184 Sqdn and operated against various targets (including V-1 sites) on the Continent until early 1944 when the 'Hurris' were replaced by the faster and more effective Hawker Typhoon.

Sea Hurricane Mk XIIB (JS327) was a Canadian-built aircraft assigned to the Royal Navy for OPERATION TORCH — the Allied landings in North Africa in November of 1942. RN aircraft, including Hurricanes, Martlets, and Fulmars, were given temporary US insignia as part of a campaign to convince everyone in the region that the operation was an all American campaign.

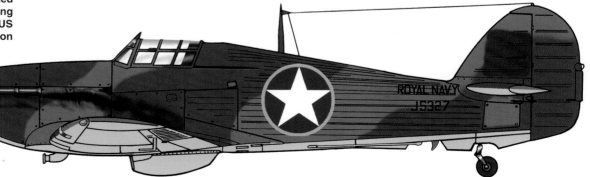

In addition to bomb pylons, the Mk IIB could be equipped with long range fuel tanks. The initial examples were non-jettisonable and unstressed for combat. The later tanks were fully combat capable and held 44 gallons of fuel. The tanks were mounted in the same location as the bomb pylons. The extra pair of outboard guns can be seen protruding from the wing leading edge just outboard of the landing light. The outer guns of the 'B' wing were often equipped with a small conical flash suppressors. The Vokes air filter was usually fitted to Hurricanes serving North Africa and South Asia. Its use meant a slightly reduced speed, however, it considerably prolonged engine life. On 9 April 1942 BE227 was shot down by A6M Zeros over China Bay during the Japanese carrier strikes on the Island of Ceylon in the Indian Ocean.

Hurricane Mk IICs of 94 Sqdn fly over the Western Desert during the latter part of 1942. The armament has been reduced from four to two cannons with the outer weapons apertures faired over (as on GO~N) or with no fairing at all on the other fighters.

The Walk Around Series Each book provides an in-depth look at the subject, inside and out, using color and black and white photographs, illustrations, and line art. 40 pages of color, 40 pages of black and white

5504 F4F Wildcat

5507 P-51D

5508 P-40 Warhawk

5509 F6F Hellcat

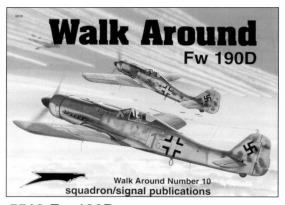

5510 Fw 190D

5511 P-47 Thunderbolt

5512 B-25 Mitchell

5513 Allison Engined Mustangs